HEINEMANN STATE STUDIES

People of Florida

Bob Knotts

D1308358

Heinemann Library
Chicago, Illinois

Designed by Heinemann Library
Page layout by Wilkinson Design
Printed and bound in the United States by
Lake Book Manufacturing, Inc.

07 06 05 04 03
10 9 8 7 6 5 4 3 2 1

**Library of Congress
Cataloging-in-Publication Data**

Knotts, Bob.
  People of Florida / Bob Knotts.
    v. cm. -- (State studies)
Includes bibliographical references and index.
Contents: Florida's people -- Population movement
-- Cultural groups --
Important Floridians.
  ISBN 1-40340-349-X -- ISBN 1-40340-565-4
(pbk.)
  1. Florida--History--Juvenile literature. 2.
Florida--Population--Juvenile literature. 3.
Ethnology--Florida--Juvenile literature. [1. Florida.]
I. Title. II.
State studies (Heinemann Library (Firm))
  F311.3 .K584 2003
  975.9--dc21
                          2002005922

Acknowledgments
The author and publishers are grateful to the
following for permission to reproduce copyright
material:

Cover photography by (top, L-R) The Granger
Collection, Steven J. Nesius/Heinemann Library,
Tony Arruza, Bettmann/Corbis, (main) Steven J.
Nesius/Heinemann Library

Title page (L-R) AP/Wide World Photos, Brown
Brothers, Bettmann/Corbis; contents page (L-R)
Mary Evans Picture Library, The Granger
Collection, Corbis; p. 4 Gianni Dagli Orti/Corbis;
pp. 5, 19, 23 Stephen J. Nesius/Heinemann
Library; pp. 5B, 11, 45 maps.com/Heinemann
Library; p. 10 Northwind Picture Archive; pp. 12T,
21, 36, 37T, 39B, 43T The Granger Collection;
p. 12B Wolfgang Kaehler/Corbis; p. 13 Mary Evans
Picture Library; p. 14 St. Augustine, Ponte Vedra &
The Beaches Visitors and Convention Bureau;
p. 15 Lee Snider/Corbis; p. 16 Frederic Remington
Art Museum; p. 17 Raymond Gehman/Corbis;
pp. 18, 38, 40, 42T Corbis; p. 20T Courtesy of the
Seminole Tribe Photographers; pp. 20B, 35, 43B
Bettmann/Corbis; p. 22 Lewis Wickers Hine/Corbis;
p. 24 Nik Wheeler/Corbis; pp. 25, 39T Brown
Brothers; p. 26 Florida State Archives; pp. 27T, 44B
Tom Ervin/AP/Wide World Photos; p. 27B Kathy
Willens/AP/Wide World Photos; p. 28 Marta Garcia;
p. 29 Marta Lavandier/AP/Wide World Photos;
pp. 30, 32 Tony Arruza; p. 31 Tony Arruza/Corbis;
p. 34 Mark E. Gibson/Corbis; p. 37B Bozidar
Vukicevic/AP/Wide World Photos; p. 41 Stock
Montage; p. 42B Rene Macura/AP/Wide World
Photos; p. 44T AFP/Corbis

Photo Research by Julie Laffin

Special thanks to Charles Tingley of the
St. Augustine Historical Society for his comments
in the preparation of this manuscript.

Every effort has been made to contact copyright
holders of any material reproduced in this book.
Any omissions will be rectified in subsequent
printings if notice is given to the publisher.

Some words are shown in bold, **like this.**
You can find out what they mean by looking
in the glossary.

Contents

Florida's People

People first started living in Florida around 12,000 years ago. Those people were called **Paleo-Indians,** and they slowly spread across Florida's land. Since that time, Florida's **demographics** have changed a lot, especially over the past 50 years. Millions of people from all over the world have come to Florida to seek a better life. Today, people from over 250 different countries live here.

Florida's first residents were Paleo-Indians. They hunted animals, like this mammoth, which lived in Florida at the time.

Because of increased immigration, Florida's Hispanic population almost doubled from 1990 to 2000.

So do people who came to Florida from the other 49 states of this country. So many people have moved to Florida that it now has the fourth largest population in the entire United States. The U.S. **census** reports that only California, Texas, and New York have larger populations.

From 1990 to 2000, Florida's population increased a great deal. The number of people

You can use this map to figure out the growth that Florida has experienced. How much has your county grown since 1940?

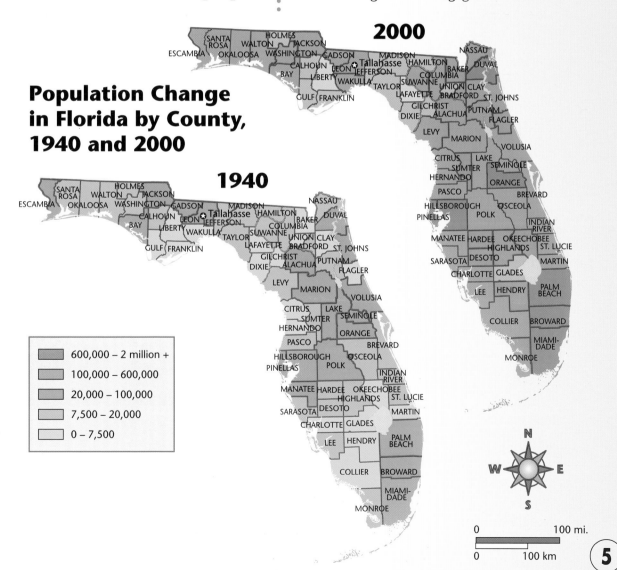

Population Change in Florida by County, 1940 and 2000

2000

1940

Legend:
- 600,000 – 2 million +
- 100,000 – 600,000
- 20,000 – 100,000
- 7,500 – 20,000
- 0 – 7,500

0   100 mi.
0   100 km

Florida's Demographics: 1990 vs. 2000

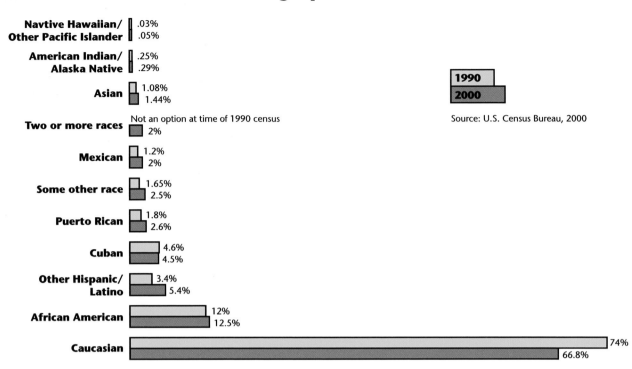

Navtive Hawaiian/ Other Pacific Islander: .03% / .05%

American Indian/ Alaska Native: .25% / .29%

Asian: 1.08% / 1.44%

Two or more races: Not an option at time of 1990 census / 2%

Mexican: 1.2% / 2%

Some other race: 1.65% / 2.5%

Puerto Rican: 1.8% / 2.6%

Cuban: 4.6% / 4.5%

Other Hispanic/ Latino: 3.4% / 5.4%

African American: 12% / 12.5%

Caucasian: 74% / 66.8%

1990
2000

Source: U.S. Census Bureau, 2000

*Florida's **demographics** have changed over the last ten years. Which group has grown the most? Which group has grown the least?*

living in the state grew from more than 12 million in 1990 to nearly 16 million in 2000. The fastest-growing counties in Florida at this time are Flagler, Wakulla, Lake, St. John's, Collier, Osceola, Pasco, Walton, and Lee. These counties are spread all around Florida, showing that growth is not concentrated in just one area.

What Is a Census?

A census is the name given to the **federal government's** effort to count every person in the United States, so we know exactly how many people live here. The census, which takes place every ten years in the United States, also tells us where these people live and some other things about who they are. The government mails out questions to homes all over the United States asking for information. People from the government also travel to communities around the country to look for information and ask questions about the people living there.

FLORIDA'S CENSUS DATA

This is what Florida's population looks like today: 65 percent of the state's people are Caucasian and non-Hispanic. That means that 65 out of every 100 Floridians have families who trace their ancestors back to European countries. Seventeen percent of Florida's people are Hispanic, from countries like Cuba, Mexico, and Nicaragua. Florida's population is also fifteen percent African American. African Americans are the second-largest minority group in the state.

A minority group is a group of people whose **ethnicity** is different from most other people living in an area. Any group of people that makes up less than half of the total population is called a minority. Any group of people that makes up more than half of the total population is called a majority.

Most people who have **immigrated** to Florida from other places have kept their own culture in this state. A culture means the language, traditions, food, music, art, beliefs, and religions of any group. Florida is home to a variety of different cultures from many different lands. Yet all of the people from these different cultures live together within this single state. All these different people and all these different cultures have made Florida an unusual and exciting state. No place else on earth is quite like Florida.

Florida's People

Most people who live in Florida are **descendants** of European settlers. Hispanics and African Americans make up the next largest groups in Florida.

Other minority groups living in Florida include people from China, Japan, Thailand, and other countries in Asia, as well as people from Haiti, Jamaica, and other Caribbean nations.

Each of these minority groups has added something special to Florida. Each has brought its own culture. Each has helped to make Florida the **diverse** place it is today.

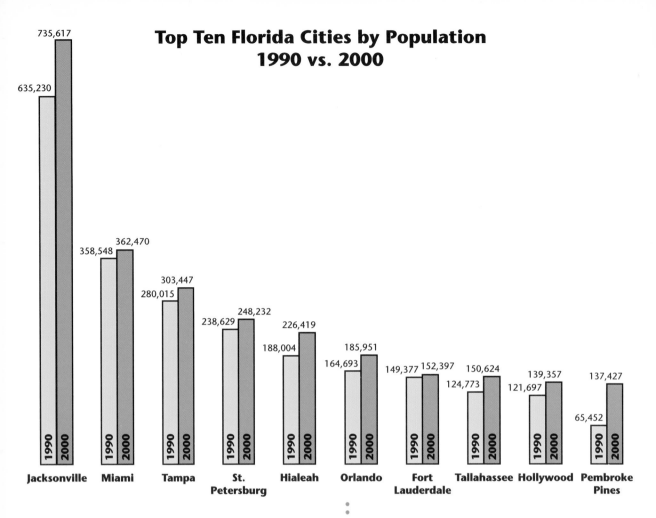

Top Ten Florida Cities by Population
1990 vs. 2000

735,617

635,230

362,470
358,548

303,447
280,015

248,232
238,629

226,419
188,004

185,951
164,693

152,397
149,377

150,624
124,773

139,357
121,697

137,427
65,452

| 1990 | 2000 | | 1990 | 2000 | | 1990 | 2000 | | 1990 | 2000 | | 1990 | 2000 | | 1990 | 2000 | | 1990 | 2000 | | 1990 | 2000 | | 1990 | 2000 | | 1990 | 2000 |

Jacksonville **Miami** **Tampa** **St. Petersburg** **Hialeah** **Orlando** **Fort Lauderdale** **Tallahassee** **Hollywood** **Pembroke Pines**

Florida's ten largest cities have grown over the past ten years. According to this graph, which city's population has grown the most?

WHERE DO FLORIDA'S PEOPLE LIVE?

The people of Florida live in different parts of the state. Many have moved into large cities, where lots of people live closely together. The most crowded area is southeast Florida. More than five million people live in this part of the state.

Other parts of Florida have very few people. Some of these areas are covered by forests or swamps. For example, very few people live in the Everglades, a huge swamp in southern Florida.

Some of Florida's counties are made up of mostly farmland or pastures used for raising cattle and horses. These areas in the northern, central, and panhandle regions of Florida have fewer people than the large cities.

If you want to meet the interesting people of Florida you must travel all around the state: to the big cities, the small towns, the farms, and the ranches. You will have to travel to the Everglades and the Florida Keys. If you do make this trip, you will hear many languages spoken. These include English, Spanish, Creole, Portuguese, Greek, Chinese, French, Hebrew, Russian, and Mikisuki. You will also learn about the foods, interests, and cultures of people from nearly everywhere in the world.

This is why many people think Florida is one of the most interesting places on earth. From the Scots of Dunedin to the Slovaks and Czechs of Slavia and Masaryktown; from the Florida Crackers to Miami's Cuban-American community; it is clear that there is **diversity** in Florida's population. Its people have made it a very special place to be.

The Florida Folk Festival

The Florida Folk Festival was started in 1953 in White Springs, Florida. People of African, Cracker, Czech, Greek, Jewish, Miccosukee, Minorcan, Seminole, and Spanish **heritage** all came together to share their music, storytelling, and dancing.

The 50th anniversary of the Florida Folk Festival was celebrated in 2002. New groups attended the festival at that time, including Acadians, Armenians, East Indians, Guatemalans, Haitians, Hawaiians, Hungarians, Irish, Peruvians, Serbians, and Trinidadians.

The **demographics** of Florida may have changed over the years, but not the willingness of the state's residents to share their own cultures and learn about the cultures of others.

Settlement of Florida

The story of Florida's settlement begins with the **Paleo-Indians.** We call them Paleo-Indians because we do not know what they called themselves. The word *paleo* means "ancient," or very old, in Greek. These people came to Florida 12,000 years ago from colder lands to the north. Because of Florida's warm weather and **abundant** food sources, they found it easier to survive.

Over time, these Paleo-Indians moved into different parts of Florida and became organized into separate groups. Among others, these included the Apalachee, Timucua, Calusa, Tequesta, Ais, Yamasee, Osochi, Ocale, Panazola, Chatot, Tocobaga, Guale, and Jeaga.

The groups we know the most about today are the Apalachee, Timucua, Calusa, and Tequesta. In northern Florida, the Apalachee and the Timucua farmed for beans, corn,

Some of Florida's early native peoples wore tattoos covering their entire bodies, like the man at left. This drawing was made in 1650.

and squash. In the south, the Calusa and the Tequesta fished and hunted. For hundreds of years, these groups were Florida's only human inhabitants.

EUROPEAN EXPLORERS

In 1513, Spanish explorers came to Florida for the first time. By 1559, French explorers had also arrived. In 1586, English soldiers came, too.

All of these countries—Spain, France, and England—were looking for lands far away from their own homes. They hoped to get rich by controlling these places and the people who lived there.

Florida at the Time of European Contact

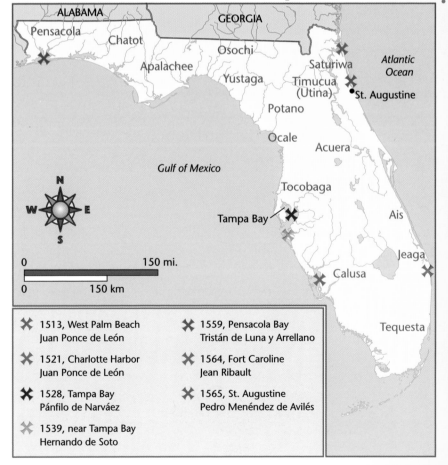

There was almost no part of early Florida that was not settled by Native Americans. This map shows the locations of Florida's Indians at the time that European explorers arrived.

Juan Ponce de León

The Spanish explorer Juan Ponce de León was the first European to come to Florida. He named the state *la Florida* after a Spanish Easter celebration called *Pascua Florida,* which means "season of flowers."

From 1509 to 1512, Ponce de León served as governor of the island of Puerto Rico. He then came to Florida looking for gold and silver. He tried to force the native peoples into slavery, and make them work for him.

On his second trip in 1521, Ponce de León was wounded during a battle with the Calusa. He died of these wounds a few days later in Cuba.

When Europeans arrived in Florida during the 1500s, they found huge cornfields and miles of trees. Much of the land was being used by early Native Americans. The Europeans thought that the land was worth fighting over. From 1559 to 1821, Spain, France, and England continued to fight over parts of the state. They built new European communities. The first European city in Florida was St. Augustine, which was founded in 1565 by the Spanish.

The Spanish had a large **influence** on Florida. The style of buildings commonly seen in Spain is still seen

The red tile roof of Flagler College in St. Augustine, Florida, shows the city's Spanish **heritage.**

in modern Florida today. Spanish-style **architecture** often has orange, rounded tiles for roofs. These buildings often have open areas, called patios, near the front door.

Spain and England continued to send more settlers to Florida from their own countries. These settlers brought diseases with them that killed many of the early native peoples, who had no **resistance** to these diseases. Constant warfare between the groups also reduced the number of Florida's native peoples. When the Spaniards first arrived in 1513 there had been more than 100,000 Native Americans in Florida; just twenty years later, there were only 11,000. Finally, in 1763—when Great Britain took control of Florida from Spain—the last of Florida's original native peoples left with the Spanish to go to Cuba or Mexico.

THE SEMINOLES ARRIVE

From about 1750 onward, a new group of Native Americans started to enter Florida. Creek Indians from what is today Georgia began to migrate to Florida in search of places to live that were not overrun by settlers. By roughly 1775, these Creek migrants were known as Seminoles. This word may have come from the Creek word *simanó-li,* meaning "runaway," or it may have come from the Spanish word *cimarrón,* meaning "wild." The Seminoles lived mostly by hunting and fishing, and built houses called *chickees,* which had thatched roofs and no walls.

This image of a Seminole leader, made around 1830, clearly shows traditional Seminole clothing. George Catlin, the artist, became famous for painting Native Americans.

These Seminoles found themselves in conflict with the settlers in Florida. Settlers wanted land that was being used by the Seminoles.

AFRICANS IN FLORIDA

The history of Africans in Florida is a long one. The first Africans arrived in the early 1500s with Spanish explorers. For example, in 1513, an African called Juan Garrido arrived in Florida with Ponce de León. By the late 1500s, more than one out of every ten people in the city of St. Augustine was African or of African **descent;** one of every five of those people was free.

In the 1700s, many slaves seeking their freedom escaped to Florida from English colonists' farms in South Carolina. These escaped slaves found freedom at Fort Mose and other small communities in northern Florida.

Fort Mose, which at that time was in territory controlled by the Spanish, was the first town in what is today the United States where African Americans were protected and allowed to have their own free community. Other former slaves found **refuge** with the Seminole Indians who lived in that area. At times, both the Seminoles

Reenactors act out the history of Fort Mose. They teach visitors about the residents' way of life.

and the escaped slaves helped the Spanish fight against the English, who controlled territory to the north. When Spain gave up control of Florida to England in 1763, most of the free blacks at Fort Mose and in the rest of northern Florida went to live in Cuba with the Spanish. Today, Fort Mose is a **national historic landmark.**

New Arrivals in Florida

When Great Britain took control of Florida, Scottish, English, and Irish settlers moved there to farm the land. Wealthy British farmers brought in African slaves to work on their large **plantations.** That is how large

*Gamble Mansion is located on what was once a large sugar **plantation** in Ellenton, Florida. It was worked by 190 slaves.*

numbers of Africans arrived in Florida for the first time: as slaves. By 1860, there were 62,000 slaves in Florida.

Most of the settlers who came to Florida, however, were not wealthy. Many of them had first moved to Georgia and Alabama, and then went to Florida when Great Britain took possession, eager to take advantage of the cheap land. These people, who were largely **subsistence** farmers, came to be known as Florida Crackers. They were called Crackers probably because of the sound their whips made while herding their cattle, tough animals that were **descendants** of the cattle originally brought to Florida by the Spanish in the 1500s. Poor but proud, the Crackers strongly believed in the value of hard work. Many of Florida's residents today are the descendants of the original Florida Crackers.

There are a number of places in Florida that are dedicated to the preservation of the original Cracker way of life. Homeland, Florida, hosts the annual Cracker Storytelling Festival. There, you can listen to stories about Florida's early settlers and their lives, and take part in a crackerwhip contest. You can also travel to Lake Kissimmee State Park, where park rangers dress as Cracker cow hunters, or cowboys, and teach about the Cracker lifestyle in Florida's frontier cattle country.

Frederic Remington, who was mostly known for his paintings of the American West, also painted several images of Florida's Cracker cow hunters. This painting was first published in Harper's Magazine in 1895.

This park ranger at Lake Kissimmee State Park is dressed as a Florida Cracker from the 1800s.

Florida even has two breeds of animals named for the Crackers: the Florida Cracker cattle and Florida Cracker horse. Both of these are descended from the animals that the original Florida Crackers depended upon to live.

Jewish People in Florida

Records show Jewish settlers living in Florida for the first time in 1763. Joseph de Palacios, Samuel Israel, and Alexander Solomon moved to Pensacola from New Orleans. They came at that time because the British allowed them to practice their religion, while the Spanish had not permitted them to do so. Throughout the 1800s, more Jewish families moved to Florida.

The first chapter of the Jewish organization called B'nai B'rith was set up in 1874 in Pensacola, Florida. B'nai B'rith is now an international group that works to support Jewish causes. The group also provides **philanthropic** services to different groups of people, regardless of their religion.

The Minorcans

New groups continued to arrive in Florida throughout the 1700s. In 1768, a British doctor convinced a group of 1,400 people—mostly from the island of Minorca, off the north-east coast of Spain—to move to New Smyrna, Florida.

He told them that if they came to Florida and worked on his land for a period of time, he would then give them their own land. A small number of Greeks and Italians also joined the Minorcans.

Many died on the ocean voyage, and more died in the years that followed due to poor working and living conditions and cruel treatment. The doctor treated the settlers like slaves, and would not let them leave. In 1777, the colony was **liberated** by the governor of Florida, who had been told of the situation. The surviving 600 colonists moved to St. Augustine, where they stayed. Many of St. Augustine's residents today are related to the Minorcan, Greek, and Italian families who traveled to Florida in 1768.

THE SEMINOLES AND THE SETTLERS

In the 1820s, Americans from other parts of the country moved south to start farms in northern Florida. As more settlers moved to Florida, they realized that the land they wanted was already being used and lived on by the

Osceola

Osceola was born around 1803 and died in 1838. He was one of Florida's greatest Native American leaders.

Osceola helped inspire Florida Seminoles to fight during the Second Seminole War, which lasted from 1835 to 1842.

Osceola encouraged the Seminoles to fight for their land against U.S. Army troops. The Seminoles won some of these fights, but Osceola was caught by the army late in 1837. He was sent to prison, where he soon died of disease.

Seminoles and the Seminole Freedmen. Seminole Freedmen were escaped slaves who lived with or near the Seminoles. The two groups formed an **alliance,** and they fought to keep their land. The U.S. Army eventually forced most Seminoles out of Florida during the Second Seminole War, which lasted from 1835 to 1842. Some Seminoles managed to **evade** the U.S. Army by retreating to the state's wildest areas, far away from other people. Even today, some Seminoles still live in the Everglades. Others live near large cities such as Fort Lauderdale, on the state's southeast coast.

This Miccosukee woman is making ***traditional*** *clothing.*

Today, the two largest Native American groups in Florida are the Miccosukee and the Seminole. There are fewer than 1,000 Miccosukees in Florida, while more than 2,000 Seminoles live here today. The Miccosukee were originally part of the Seminole Nation, but they decided they wanted to be a separate group. After 1957, they formed their own tribe. In 1962, the Miccosukee were finally recognized by the **federal government** as the Miccosukee Tribe of Indians of Florida.

Both groups welcome non-Native Americans to visit them and learn about their culture. For example, the Ah-Tah-Thi-Ki Museum, on the Big Cypress Reservation of the Seminoles, teaches both visitors and Seminole students about Seminole history, customs, legends, and languages through a number of different **exhibits** and **artifacts.** *Ah-tah-thi-ki* is a word that means "to learn" in the

Mikisuki language, one of two languages spoken by the Seminoles.

The Seminoles also print their own newspaper, which is called the *Seminole Tribune*. The newspaper writes about issues important to many Seminoles, such as the preservation of their **heritage** and the advancement of businesses. It also recognizes people in the community for their achievements.

An editor looks over the latest edition of the Seminole Tribune, *the newspaper published by the Seminole Tribe.*

The **influence** of Florida's native peoples on the state of Florida is strong today, even outside of their communities. The names of cities such as Miami and Micanopy come from languages spoken by Native Americans, and Florida farmers continue to grow crops first planted by Native Americans, including corn, beans, and squash.

THE CIVIL WAR AND AFRICAN AMERICANS

During the **Civil War,** which lasted from 1861 to 1865, most of Florida fought with rebelling Southern forces

After the Civil War, thousands of African Americans became sharecroppers. The majority lived in poverty, as this photo illustrates.

against the North. When the South lost the war in 1865, Florida's slave owners were forced to set about 70,000 slaves free. Some of these African Americans moved to small towns; others went to large cities. Some stayed on **plantations** where they had previously been slaves, and were paid for their labor, but not all landowners had money to pay for this work. All of Florida's former slaves were faced with the difficulty of making a new life in a world where few of them owned their own land or had received any type of education. They often faced **racism** and **discrimination.**

Mary McLeod Bethune

Mary McLeod Bethune, born in 1875 to former slaves, is one of the most important African Americans in Florida history.

Bethune was a teacher from 1895 to 1904. In 1904, she started the Daytona Normal and Industrial Institute for Girls on Florida's east coast. She had only $1.50 to do this, and the school was very poor. Students used burned strips of wood for pencils, writing with the charcoal tips. The school's kitchen supplies and chairs were taken from piles of trash, then cleaned and fixed.

In 1923, Bethune's school joined with the Cookman Institute and changed its named to Bethune-Cookman College. Today this school is located in Daytona Beach, on Florida's east coast.

Bethune later became so famous and well respected as a teacher that she advised four U.S. presidents. She was also the only black woman present at the founding of the United Nations.

Bethune died in 1955.

Many former slaves became sharecroppers. In this system, a landowner would provide the sharecropper with the land and machinery necessary to produce crops. In exchange, the sharecropper would then pay the landowner "rent" by giving him or her a portion of the crops that were grown on that land.

NEW INDUSTRIES BRING NEW IMMIGRANTS

After the **Civil War** ended, a man named Vicente Martínez Ybor moved his cigar factory from Cuba to Key West, and then to the Tampa area. Many Cubans employed in his factory came with him. Workers from Italy and Spain also found work in the cigar factories of Tampa, as did a number of Florida Crackers. More cigar workers from these different cultural groups continued to arrive in Tampa through the 1920s. Some of them formed social clubs that provided them with medical care, **benefits,** recreation, and education. Some of these clubs—such as the L'Unione Italiana (Italian Club)—still exist to this day. Today, many residents of Ybor City—a part of Tampa—are the **descendants** of these Cuban, Italian, Spanish, and Cracker tobacco workers.

The social clubs joined by Ybor City's tobacco workers made sure that the workers' working conditions were clean and safe, rarities at that time.

Born and Bred Floridians

By 1880, Florida's population had grown tremendously. In that year, the state had more than 269,000 residents. More than 60 percent of those people—six out of every ten—had been born in Florida. Since that time, the state has never again had so many of its people born within its borders. Today, most people who live in Florida were actually born in other places.

Another industry in Florida that changed the face of its inhabitants was the sponge industry. In the 1890s, a businessman hired a Greek sponge merchant, John Cocoris, to help him harvest the sponges that could be found in the waters near Tarpon Springs, on Florida's west coast. At that time, certain parts of Greece had a flourishing sponge industry, and the businessman wanted someone who was familiar with that industry to help him develop the business in Florida. Cocoris sent for his brother and friends, who were experienced sponge workers in Greece. They began to harvest Florida's sponges. After 1905, hundreds more Greeks **immigrated** to the area to work in the sponge industry. Their families came with them.

Today, one-third of Tarpon Springs's 21,000 citizens are of Greek descent. These

Sponges are still sold from the docks in Tarpon Springs today.

*These Greek-American children, marching in the yearly Epiphany parade in Tarpon Springs, are wearing **traditional** Greek clothing.*

descendants still practice the Orthodox Greek faith brought by their ancestors. Each year on January 6 the Greek community celebrates the **Epiphany.** As a part of the celebration, a weighted cross is thrown into the ocean, and high school boys dive in after it. The boy who finds the cross is said to be blessed with good luck for an entire year. The Greek Cultural Center also sponsors events that celebrate the history of Tarpon Springs's Greek **heritage.**

DEVELOPMENT ENCOURAGES NEW SETTLEMENT

During the 1890s, railroads were built to connect Florida to the rest of the country. People were able to come and visit Florida easily. Some of these visitors decided to move to Florida to live.

Around 1900, workers began to dry out some of Florida's swampland. Then they built new houses, businesses,

Henry Morrison Flagler

Henry Morrison Flagler, born in 1830 in Hopewell, New York, was one of the most important people in Florida's history. He built many of the railroads and hotels that helped make this state into what it is today.

Flagler visited Jacksonville in 1878. He knew that Florida could become very popular with visitors from colder states to the north because of its warm climate. Flagler was a very rich man, and he paid workers to build railroads along the entire east coast of Florida. In 1894, his company laid railroad tracks all the way to West Palm Beach, in southeast Florida. In the neighboring town of Palm Beach he built two expensive hotels, hoping to attract tourists.

Two years later, Flagler's railroad ran even farther south to what was then a very small town on the Atlantic Ocean. He built streets, water and power systems, and started a newspaper there. The people in this town wanted to name the community "Flagler," after the man who had given them so much. However, Flagler turned down the honor and asked that they use a Native American name instead—*Miami*—which they did.

Finally, Flagler built a railroad across the Florida Keys. The Keys are a group of small islands, more than 100 miles long, at the southern tip of the state. The railroad no longer runs through the Keys. Instead, there is a road to take people through the Keys by automobile. This road uses the same path originally cleared for Flagler's railroad.

Flagler died in 1913. He made a lasting contribution to Florida's growth.

and roads. This helped spark the **Florida Land Boom** of the 1920s. People from all around the country came to try and make a profit buying and selling Florida's land. South Florida especially grew at that time; Miami's population more than tripled!

Pilots trained for World War II combat in Florida. In the 1940s, there were more than 40 airfields in Florida at which pilots were training for war.

World War II, which lasted from 1939 to 1945, started Florida's biggest period of change and movement. Thousands of American soldiers trained in Florida because of the state's good weather. After the war, many of these people brought their families to live in Florida. They built homes with money that the **federal government** provided to help former military men and women.

By 1950, the **census** counted 2.7 million people living in Florida. This included older Americans, who had retired from their jobs in other states and moved to Florida to enjoy the warm weather. Today, one of almost every five people living in Florida is retired.

THE JEWISH POPULATION INCREASES

During the 1950s, Florida had more jobs—and more types of jobs—than ever before. This strong economy helped attract Americans to Florida from other states.

More Jewish people moved to Florida, especially from northeastern states. Today, at least 750,000 Jews live in

In Miami Beach, the Holocaust Memorial stands as a symbol of the Jews who were victims of the Nazis during World War II. Holocaust survivors work at the memorial's information booth.

Florida. Most live near Miami, Fort Lauderdale, or West Palm Beach. Miami-Dade County has the third largest Jewish community in the United States.

A number of Jewish people who lived through the **Holocaust** have made their homes in Florida. The Holocaust Memorial stands in Miami Beach, a community along the Atlantic Ocean in southeast Florida. This memorial was built to remember the millions of innocent Jews who were killed during World War II by the **Nazis.**

Isaac Bashevis Singer

Isaac Bashevis Singer was a Polish-born Jewish writer who lived from 1904 to 1991. He made his home in Miami Beach, and taught college students nearby.

Singer wrote stories, books, and plays about Jewish life in Poland. He won the **Nobel prize** for literature in 1978 for his work.

Singer loved Florida. He called Miami Beach the "city of the future." He is one of many writers who have lived and worked in the state of Florida.

*This man in Little Havana waves the Cuban flag. Cuban Americans are limited in the amount of money they can send to their relatives in Cuba by the U.S. government, because the government does not agree with many of Cuba's **political policies**.*

A NEW WAVE OF CUBAN IMMIGRATION

In 1959, Fidel Castro took power in Cuba, an island nation only 90 miles from Key West. Since many Cubans wanted more freedom than Castro allowed, or disagreed with the way he was running the country, they moved to Florida. About half a million Cubans moved to the Miami area from 1960 to 1980. In 1980, another 100,000 Cubans came as a part of what was called the Mariel Boatlift. At that time, Castro opened the port of Mariel and permitted Cuban citizens to emigrate to the United States.

Soon, people from all over Latin America started to move to southeast Florida. They came from Venezuela, Colombia, Nicaragua, Brazil, Costa Rica, El Salvador, Guatemala, and Peru.

Florida's largest minority group is made up of Hispanic people. More than 2.6 million Floridians are also Hispanics. Southeast Florida is an area where a lot of Hispanics have chosen to live. Miami-Dade County is home to 1.3 million Hispanic people, and 650,000 of them are Cuban. Almost 272,000 Hispanics live in and around Fort Lauderdale in Broward County. Many

Joe Carollo, a Cuban-American, served as mayor of Miami.

government leaders in southeast Florida are a part of this minority. For example, Miami has had several Cuban-American mayors.

Orange County, located in the middle of Florida (and home to Orlando and Disney World), also has a large Hispanic population. Between 1990 and 2000, Orange County's Hispanic population grew by 159 percent. Now, almost one out of every five people in this county is Hispanic.

There are newspapers and magazines published in Spanish in Florida, and there are dozens of Spanish radio stations. Spanish television stations are also very popular. Some Spanish television programs are filmed in Miami and later seen around the United States and Latin America.

Florida's Hispanic community sponsors festivals. The largest is called *Calle Ocho*, which is named after the street where it is held in Miami's Little Havana

At the Calle Ocho festival people can eat food, like this paella, from all over the Hispanic world. People come from as far away as Europe and Asia to attend the festival.

neighborhood. *Calle Ocho* means "Eighth Street" in Spanish. Every year, hundreds of thousands of people go to the Calle Ocho festival. They sing, dance, and eat food from countries all over Latin America and parts of the Caribbean.

Little Havana is an area of Miami where thousands of Cuban Americans live and work. Recently, more and more people from other Latin American countries have moved to Little Havana, too. Today, 49 percent of the people who live in Little Havana are Cuban. The rest of the people living there are from other Latin American countries, including Colombia and Venezuela.

Hispanics in Florida have changed the popular music heard there, across the United States, and around the world. Today, Miami is still the place where many Hispanic musicians record and perform their music. Their efforts have helped make Latin music among the most popular music in the world today.

Because there are so many Hispanics in southeast Florida, Miami and Fort Lauderdale have become very important places for doing business with Latin American companies and governments. Banks and other southeast Florida companies that handle money do lots of business with Latin American countries.

IMMIGRANTS FROM THE CARIBBEAN

People from the Caribbean, or West Indian, islands make up another large minority group in Florida. They have **influenced** the communities where they moved in large numbers. More than 492,000 Floridians have come from the Caribbean, including Haiti, Jamaica, the Bahamas, Trinidad and Tobago, and the U.S. Virgin Islands, a U.S. territory. Cuba is also one of the Caribbean islands.

Bahamian Americans celebrate at the Goombay Festival, held in Miami.

People have also come to Florida from Jamaica, Barbados, the Dominican Republic, and Haiti. Haiti is one of the world's poorest countries. Large numbers of Haitians first started to come to Florida during the 1970s hoping to find better jobs, better education, and freedom from **persecution.** They continued to emigrate to Florida throughout the 1980s and 1990s.

More than 267,000 Haitians now live in Florida. Thousands of them live in a part of Miami called Little Haiti. The store signs are in Creole—the common language of Haitians—and Creole is heard everywhere as people talk. The Creole language uses some French words, but sounds very different from French.

Restaurants in Little Haiti serve Haitian foods. Shops sell fruits that are popular in Haiti, including plantains and mangos. Haitians also have their own newspaper in southeast Florida, called the *Kiskeya Herald.*

This Haitian-American father and daughter are working in their store in Miami's Little Haiti neighborhood.

Key West Conchs

Bahamians of British or African descent moved to Key West during the 1800s. They were called "conchs," probably because they often depended on a local shellfish called conch for food. Today, the word "conch" is used to describe anyone who is a native of Key West.

On April 23, 1982, the people of Key West established their own separate nation called the Conch Republic and announced that they were going to **secede** from the Florida Keys. They did this because they were angry that the U.S. government had set up a roadblock between the Keys and the mainland; this was hurting the tourist industry, on which much of Key West depends. After Key West announced its secession the government took the roadblock away. Each year on April 23, residents of Key West celebrate the anniversary of the founding of their republic as Conch Republic Day.

In 2001, the people of North Miami elected a Haitian American as their mayor: Josaphat Celestin. He is the first Haitian-American mayor of a large city in the United States. Many of the city government's leaders, called council members, are also Haitian Americans.

Jamaican Americans also live in Florida. Like Haiti, Jamaica is an island nation that lies southeast of Florida. People from Jamaica make up the second-largest group of Floridians from the Caribbean. More than 163,000 Jamaicans live in Florida.

Florida's economy benefits from all the business conducted with these nearby islands. So many companies work in the Caribbean islands that the *Miami Herald* newspaper runs a separate Caribbean report in its business pages every Monday. This report tells

*At the Splendid China theme park in Orlando, **traditional** Chinese dancers entertain the crowd. The theme park recreates some of China's most famous landmarks, such as the **Great Wall,** but on a much smaller scale.*

Florida's businesspeople about changes happening in the governments and companies of the Caribbean islands.

ASIAN AMERICANS

Florida's Asian-American population has been growing quickly in recent years. In 1990, Asian Americans made up 1.2 percent of Florida's total population (154,302 people); in 2000, they made up 17 percent of the total population (266,256 people). Of the people who described themselves as Asian during Florida's last **census,** the families of 27 percent of them have come from India.

The Indian community in Florida more than doubled in population between 1990 and 2000. There are more than 23,000 Indians just in Broward and Miami-Dade Counties. There are enough people with Indian **heritage** in southeast Florida that one of India's most important **Hindu** leaders—Jagadguru Shankaracharya Swami Divyanand Teerth—visited Coral Springs in 2001.

The second-largest group within Florida's Asian-American population is from the Philippines. More than 50,000

Filipinos currently live in Florida. There are also families who have come from China, Vietnam, Korea, and Japan.

THE FLORIDA OF TODAY

As you now know, people from all over the world have contributed their hard work, new ideas, and **diverse** cultures to Florida, and this has shaped the state over many centuries. These people remind us that Florida is much more than just sunshine and pretty white beaches. The most important part of Florida is its people—the people who lived here in the past and those who live here today.

Each year, thousands of new citizens are proud to call Florida their new home. These people are pledging allegiance to the United States at the Orange Bowl Stadium in Miami.

Important Floridians

The following people are among those who have helped make Florida a great state throughout its long history. Many of these people were born in Florida, and some moved to the state and became Floridians later in life. All of them have helped shape the Sunshine State.

Adderley, Julian "Cannonball" (1928–1975), musician. Adderley is considered by music experts to be one of the best saxophone players who ever lived. Born in Tampa, Florida, Adderley's exciting jazz performances thrilled audiences around the world.

Amos, Wallace "Wally," Jr. (1936–), businessman. Amos was born in Tallahassee. In 1975, he founded the Famous Amos Chocolate Chip Cookie Company. Many movie stars loved these cookies. Amos sold millions of them and became wealthy.

Audubon, John James (1785–1851), artist. Audubon was an artist who studied and drew birds in great detail. Though he was not born in Florida, he traveled to Key West to watch the local Florida birds and to draw them in their natural **habitats.**

John James Audubon

Bethune, Mary McLeod (1875–1955), social reformer and educator. *See page 21.*

Broward, Napoleon Bonaparte (1857–1910), politician. Elected governor in 1904, Broward helped pass laws that dried out part of the Everglades so the land could be developed and more people could live in southern Florida. Today, one of the most populated counties in the state is named for him: Broward County, which is home to Fort Lauderdale. Broward was born in 1857 in Duval County.

Carlton, Steve (1944–), baseball player. Carlton was one of the best pitchers in baseball history. Born in Miami, Florida, he won 329 games in 24 major league seasons. Carlton was **inducted** into the Baseball Hall of Fame in Cooperstown, New York in 1994.

Charles, Ray (1930–), musician. Ray Charles was one of the most famous singers and pianists of the 1950s and 1960s, and still performs today. Charles is famous for singing such tunes as "Hit the Road, Jack" and "America the Beautiful." Charles grew up in Greenville, Florida, and began playing piano there at the age of five.

Mary McLeod Bethune

Ray Charles

Hernando de Soto

De Soto, Hernando (1496–1542), explorer. De Soto was born in Spain. In 1539, he brought Spanish soldiers to explore Florida. They were searching for silver and gold, but did not find any. In 1541, he became the first European to see the Mississippi River.

Douglas, Marjory Stoneman (1890–1998), author and environmentalist. Although born in Minnesota, Douglas later moved to Florida in 1915 and wrote about the Everglades, the huge body of water that covers much of southern Florida. She helped lead the fight to create Everglades National Park and to keep the Everglades from being sold to developers. She died in 1998 at the age of 108.

Dunaway, Faye (1941–), actress. Dunaway is a famous actress, and was especially well-known during the 1960s and 1970s. Her movies include *Bonnie and Clyde*, *Chinatown*, and *Network*. She won an **Academy Award** for *Network* and still acts in movies today. Dunaway was born in Bascom, Florida.

Evert, Chris (1954–), tennis player. Evert was one of the most successful female tennis players during the 1970s and 1980s. Born in Fort Lauderdale, Florida, Evert began playing tennis at age six and later won 157 tennis titles.

Ferre, Maurice (1935–), politician. Ferre was the first Hispanic mayor of a major U.S. city. Born in Puerto Rico, Ferre was appointed mayor of Miami in 1973 and was elected to that office later the same year. Ferre was elected every two years after that until 1985. He helped improve Miami's downtown area.

Flagler, Henry Morrison (1830–1913), businessman and entrepreneur. *See page 25.*

Gooden, Dwight (1964–), baseball player. Gooden was a baseball pitcher known during the 1980s as "Dr. K." In baseball, "K" means a strikeout. He was the youngest player to win the National League's highest honor for pitchers, the Cy Young Award. He was born in Tampa.

Henry Morrison Flagler

Gorrie, John (1803–1855), doctor and inventor. John Gorrie was a doctor who lived in Apalachicola, on Florida's northern coast on the Gulf of Mexico. Gorrie thought his patients would get better faster without Florida's heat. He built an ice machine during the 1840s to cool his patients' rooms. This led to the invention of air conditioning. Gorrie was born in South Carolina.

Ernest Hemingway

Hemingway, Ernest (1899–1961), author. Hemingway was one of the 20th century's greatest writers. Hemingway is famous for books such as *A Farewell to Arms* and *The Old Man and the Sea*. Though born in Illinois, he wrote many of his works at a home in Key West, Florida. This home is now open to the public, who can see how Hemingway lived and worked.

Hurston, Zora Neale (1903–1960), author. Hurston was an African-American writer. Her stories looked at life in the

Zora Neale Hurston

small towns of Florida where only African Americans lived. Her best-known book is *Their Eyes Were Watching God*, which she wrote in 1937. She was born in Eatonville.

Johnson, James Weldon (1871–1938), poet and diplomat. Born in Jacksonville, Johnson was an African American who graduated from Atlanta University in 1894. With his brother, he wrote the song "Lift Every Voice and Sing." In 1901, he and his brother moved to New York and wrote over 200 songs for Broadway musicals. In his later life, he became a leader in the **NAACP** and a **consul** to several countries in South and Central America.

Lewis, Abraham Lincoln (A.L.) (1865–?), businessman. In 1935, Lewis, who owned the Afro-American Life Insurance Company in Jacksonville, set up American Beach on Amelia Island. This was the first beach in Florida that was open to African Americans. Before this time, they were not allowed to enjoy beaches because many white people in Florida in the early 1900s did not think blacks and whites should go to the same places. They believed in **segregation.** Lewis was Florida's first African-American millionaire.

Mallory, Stephen R. (1812–1873), politician and naval leader. During the **Civil War,** which was fought from 1861 to 1865, Mallory became Secretary of the Navy for the Southern forces fighting against President Abraham Lincoln's Northern army. Before the war, he was a United States senator from Florida. Mallory was born in Trinidad, a country in the Caribbean.

Martinez, Bob (1934–), politician. In 1986, Martinez became the first Hispanic governor of Florida since Spanish colonial days. A former mayor of Tampa, he was only the second person from the Republican Party elected governor since the Civil War. He was born in Tampa.

Menéndez de Avilés, Pedro (1519–1574), admiral and governor of Florida. As an early Spanish soldier in Florida, Menéndez de Avilés founded the city of St. Augustine in 1565. St. Augustine was the first permanent European community in what became the United States. Because of his skill as a soldier, Menéndez de Avilés helped make sure St. Augustine was not destroyed.

Pedro Menéndez de Avilés

Merrill, Charles Edward (1885–1956), banker. In 1914, Merrill started a small company that helped people make more money by **investing** it into businesses. Merrill's company grew to become the largest company of this kind in the world, then called Merrill Lynch, Pierce, Fenner & Beane. He was born in Green Cove Springs.

Morrison, Jim (1943–1971), singer and songwriter. Jim Morrison was one of the most famous singers and songwriters of the late 1960s. Born in Melbourne, Florida, Morrison started a band called The Doors.

Narváez, Panfilo de (1478–1528), explorer. This soldier was born in Spain. In 1528, he landed in Florida with his army near Tampa Bay on the Gulf of Mexico to explore the area. But attacks by native peoples and storms killed many of his soldiers. He later drowned in the Gulf of Mexico.

Osceola (1804–1838), Native American leader. *See page 18.*

Pennekamp, John D. (1897–1978), environmentalist. John Pennekamp helped to create Everglades National Park, as well as a state park that was named for him on the island south of Miami called Key Largo. That park, called the John Pennekamp Coral Reef State Park, is popular with scuba divers and snorkelers. It was the first underwater park in the United States. Pennekamp was born in Ohio, but moved to Florida in the 1920s. He is often called the "Father of the Everglades."

Osceola

Pepper, Claude (1900–1989), politician. Born in Alabama, Pepper later became a famous Florida lawmaker. He was a Florida senator from 1936 to 1950, and then became a U.S. congressman in 1962. He was best known for helping to make life better for senior citizens.

Petty, Tom (1953–), singer, songwriter. Petty is a rock singer who also plays guitar. He formed a band in 1975 called Tom Petty and the Heartbreakers. Petty became very popular for his music. He was born in Gainesville.

Poitier, Sidney (1927–), actor. Poitier won an **Academy Award** in 1963 for his role in the movie *Lilies of the Field.*

Sidney Poitier

He was the first African-American actor to receive that award. Born into a Bahamian **heritage** in Miami, Florida, he is famous for playing roles that looked at the problems of African Americans in the U.S. Some of his other movies include *Guess Who's Coming to Dinner* and *A Raisin in the Sun*.

Ponce de León, Juan (1460–1521), explorer. *See page 12.*

Juan Ponce de León

Randolph, Asa Philip (1889–1979), social activist. Randolph was an African American who helped other African Americans improve their lives at work in the United States. Randolph convinced Presidents Franklin D. Roosevelt and Harry S. Truman to offer African Americans a fair chance to be hired for higher-paying government work. In 1957, he became vice president of a national group called the AFL-CIO, which helps protect the rights of workers. Randolph was born in Crescent City, Florida.

Rawlings, Marjorie Kinnan (1896–1953), author. Born in Washington, D.C., Rawlings later moved to northern Florida and became a famous writer. In 1939, she won the **Pulitzer prize** award for her book *The Yearling*, which was about a young Cracker boy in Florida. This book was later made into a movie.

Marjorie Kinnan Rawlings

Reno, Janet (1938–), lawyer and public official. In 1993, Reno became the first female attorney general of the United States. This is the country's most important law enforcement job. Reno worked in this job for eight years, until 2001, under President Bill Clinton. She was born in Miami.

Reynolds, Burt (1936–), actor. Reynolds became famous in 1972 for his part in the movie *Deliverance*. Reynolds was most popular during the 1970s and 1980s, but one of his recent movies was *All Dogs Go to Heaven*, in which he provided the voice for the cartoon dog, Charlie. He has lived in Florida for most of his life.

Robinson, David (1965–), basketball player. Robinson is a basketball star with the San Antonio Spurs. He was Rookie of the Year for the National Basketball Association (NBA) in 1990. Born in Key West, he was on three U.S. Olympic teams.

David Robinson

Singer, Isaac Bashevis (1904–1991), author. *See page 27.*

Smith, Edmund Kirby (1824–1865), **Civil War** general. During the Civil War, Kirby Smith served as a general for the South. He was born in St. Augustine.

Thagard, Norman E. (1943–), astronaut. Thagard has been in space five times. His most recent mission was on board the Russian space station *Mir*. Thagard was born in Marianna, Florida, and grew up in Jacksonville.

Isaac Bashevis Singer

Yulee, David Levy (1810–1886), lawyer and politician. Yulee was born in the West Indies, but later practiced law in St. Augustine. He was Florida's first senator, and the first Jewish senator in the United States. Florida's Levy County is named for him.

Map of Florida

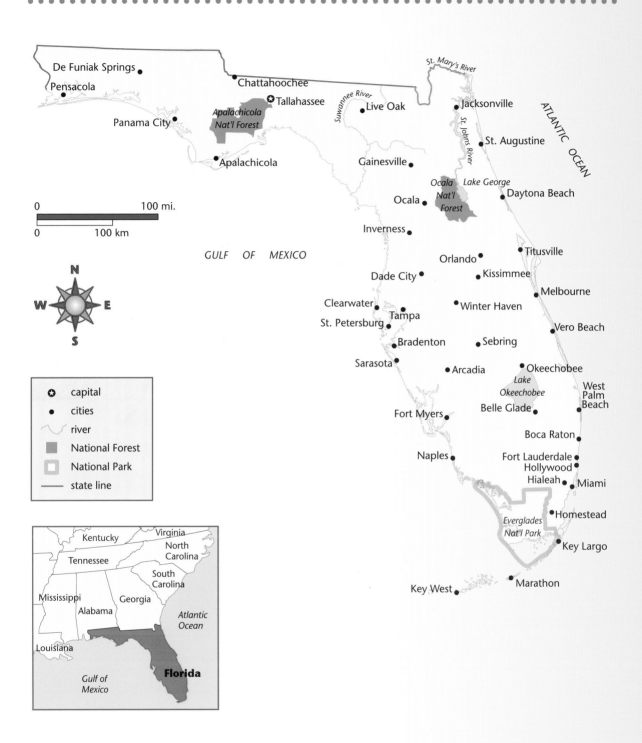

0   100 mi.

0   100 km

GULF OF MEXICO

N
W E
S

De Funiak Springs
Pensacola
Chattahoochee
Tallahassee
Apalachicola Nat'l Forest
Panama City
Apalachicola
Suwannee River
Live Oak
St. Mary's River
Jacksonville
ATLANTIC OCEAN
St. Johns River
St. Augustine
Gainesville
Ocala Nat'l Forest
Lake George
Daytona Beach
Ocala
Inverness
Titusville
Orlando
Kissimmee
Melbourne
Dade City
Winter Haven
Clearwater
Tampa
St. Petersburg
Vero Beach
Bradenton
Sebring
Sarasota
Arcadia
Okeechobee
Lake Okeechobee
West Palm Beach
Belle Glade
Fort Myers
Boca Raton
Naples
Fort Lauderdale
Hollywood
Hialeah
Miami
Homestead
Everglades Nat'l Park
Key Largo
Key West
Marathon

Legend

- ⊗ capital
- • cities
- river
- National Forest
- National Park
- state line

Inset map:

Kentucky
Virginia
Tennessee
North Carolina
South Carolina
Mississippi
Georgia
Alabama
Atlantic Ocean
Louisiana
Florida
Gulf of Mexico

Glossary

abundant plentiful

Academy Award honor given out each year for excellence in movies

alliance agreement between two or more people or groups to help one another

architecture style of building

artifact object made and used by humans long ago

benefits services, usually healthcare, that a company or group provides to its members

census effort made by the government to count each citizen of the United States

Civil War war fought from 1861 to 1865 between the North and the South

consul government representative to a foreign nation

demographics having to do with the different kinds of people who live within the same area

descend to come from originally

discrimination unfair treatment based on ignorance

diverse describes something made up of many different parts or many different kinds of things

Epiphany Christian religious service that celebrates the coming of the Magi, pilgrims who were said to have been the first to recognize Jesus

ethnicity having to do with groups of people who are classed by racial, national, tribal, religious, linguistic (language-oriented), or cultural backgrounds

evade to slip away from

exhibit display in a museum

federal government government which operates out of Washington, D.C., and which makes decisions that affect all states

Florida Land Boom period of time in south Florida from the early- to mid-1920s when land was bought and sold for huge prices

Great Wall giant wall constructed of dirt, stone, and brick in China between the seventh and fourth centuries B.C.E. The wall was built to keep invaders out. While much of it is in ruins today, at one time it ran for 4,500 miles.

habitat place where a plant or animal naturally lives and grows

heritage having to do with the history of one's family or people

Hindu person who follows the main religion in India, Hinduism

Holocaust mass killing of Jews by the Nazis during World War II

immigrant person who moves from one country to another to live

induct to nominate someone for admittance into a group

influence affect

invest to give money to a company to spend on its growth; if the company does well, it will give back more money to the people who invest in it

liberate to free

NAACP (National Association for the Advancement of Colored People)

46